THE CARNINGLI WALKS

A walkers' guide to the Newport,
Nevern & Moylgrove Area
of North Pembrokeshire

Published by

CARNINGLI RURAL INITIATIVE
Ridgeway House, Market Street, Newport,
Pembrokeshire SA42 OPH. Telephone: 01239 820235

CONTENTS Page

© Carningli Rural Initiative 1995

Editor: Brian John

Walks research: Robin Evans, Peter Harwood and David Vaughan

Line drawings: Leon Olin

Photography: John Havard. Peregrine (page 5): Michael Betts.

Cover photograph and Ceibwr (page 8): Brace Harvatt Associates

Design: Brace Harvatt Associates

Typesetting: Helen Evans and Inger John

Print: Haven Colourprint

Published with the generous support of the Welsh Development Agency and the Pembrokeshire Coast National Park Authority

1st edition 1995

ISBN: 0 9524071 0 8

INTRODUCTION

This booklet has been created by the Carningli Rural Initiative (CRI), with generous financial support from the Welsh Development Agency (WDA), in order to encourage the public enjoyment of the magnificent network of footpaths which exists in the Newport and Nevern area. Over the last few years a system of more than 66 km of footpaths has been created, for the most part utilising public rights of way but sometimes including private sections made available by landowners. The walking routes also include a number of bridleways, sections of the Pembrokeshire Coast Path, and stretches of quiet public roads.

On many of the footpaths the Prembrokeshire Coast National Park Authority (NPA) has contributed to the Carningli Walks Project by installing signposts and waymarks which are unique to the local area, clearing sections of previously under-used footpaths, and building stiles and steps in a number of locations. As a result of the co-operation between the local community, the NPA and the WDA, the area now has a network of footpaths which is second to none, serving as a reminder of the maze of footpaths, bridleways and by-ways used by the people of the Barony of Cemaes in days gone by.

The area which is dominated by the impressive rocky summit of Carningli lies entirely within the Pembrokeshire Coast National Park. The wild rugged coastline, Traeth Mawr (Big Beach), and the Nevern Estuary are well known to many thousands of holiday-makers who walk the coast path and who enjoy the local holiday facilities. However, the inland area is one of Pembrokeshire's best kept secrets, with gentle wooded valleys, extensive woodlands, windswept moorlands and high mountain crags, all on an intimate and accessible scale.

Pentre Ifan Cromlech.

Scattered throughout the Carningli area are the megalithic monuments which are permanent reminders of an ancient past. The first farmers were the Neolithic people who built the burial chambers or cromlechs at Newport, Moylgrove and Pentre Ifan. Later came the Bronze Age tribes who used the upland "ridgeways" during their trading expeditions and who left a legacy of standing stones and burial mounds. The Iron Age farmers who followed them built heavily defended forts on hill summits, coastal promontories and river valley spurs. The most impressive hill fort in the area is on the summit of Carningli itself.

Over the last two thousand years the landscape has seen many changes, including those introduced by the Normans who built the local castles at Newport and Nevern and who created the town of Newport. Fishing, coastal trading and lime burning activities have all left traces along the coastline, but inland the man-made landscape has been fashioned above all else by 5,000 years of agriculture, based for the most part upon stock rearing and (in recent decades) dairy farming. Agriculture remains the principal industry of the area today, although tourism is now an important feature of the local economy.

TOWN AND COUNTRY

Newport is a town by charter, though its population is only a little over 1,000. It was laid out as a garrison town 800 years ago and still retains its original street pattern. There are traces of old woollen and corn mills, all of which were driven by water power. The parish Church of St Mary has a squat and solid Norman-style tower. The remains of the Norman castle overlook the town. Originally moated with a drawbridge leading to the entrance and fitted with a portcullis, the castle was partly rebuilt as a house in the middle of the last century. It remains the property of the Lady Marcher of Cemais, a successor to the Norman barons who settled here in the early Middle Ages. The house is now lived in by a tenant and is not open to the public.

Trefdraeth, meaning the town on the beach, is the original Welsh name for Newport. In spite of the Norman Conquest, and the anglicisation that followed, the town has managed to retain its Welsh character and culture, and Welsh is still the main language of the town and its surrounding area.

Until comparatively recent times Newport, benefitting from the shelter provided by the estuary of the River Nevern, was an important trading port. Signs of its long seafaring tradition can be seen in the disused lime kilns and store-houses on the Parrog. Sailing ships were built at several sites on the shores of the estuary. The last large warehouse on the riverside is now the headquarters of the Boat Club.

Overlooking Newport and the surrounding countryside is Carningli, "the Mount of Angels", the northernmost peak of the Preseli Mountains. From its summit on a clear day you may see the mountains of Snowdonia and the Wicklow Hills in Ireland. Carningli is a prominent reference point for all the walks. Legend has it that the Irish monk, St Brynach, who built his cell at Nevern, regularly climbed to the top of Carningli to commune with the Angels.

The hamlet of Nevern (Nanhyfer), two miles inland, has at its centre St Brynach's Church where an avenue of yew trees flanks the entrance path. Several of these trees, the "bleeding yews", drip with sap which is blood-red in colour. Beside the church is the eleventh century Celtic Cross on top of which according to local tradition, the first cuckoo of summer sings. Nevern is one of the nodal points for the Carningli Walks.

Moylgrove (Trewyddel) is a steep hillside village close to Ceibwr Bay with its dramatic cliff scenery. There are a number of hamlets within the Carningli Walks area at Felindre Farchog, on the A 487 trunk road, and at Cilgwyn in the broad amphitheatre of the Clydach Valley. Other smaller settlement clusters are to be found on Ffordd Cilgwyn and Ffordd Bedd Morris.

WILDLIFE

The coastline of the Newport-Nevern-Moylgrove area is immensely varied, including sections of steep cliffs, quiet estuarine mud flats, sandy beaches and long, steep coastal slopes. Some of the highest cliffs in Wales are to be found within a few kilometres of Moylgrove and there are stretches of man-made cliffs to the west of Newport where the old sea quarries were worked for centuries to provide the building materials for the houses and quays of Newport and Cwm-yr-Eglwys.

Many stretches of the coastal cliffs abound with bird life, and attract bird-watchers during the summer months. However, the cliffs assume a wild beauty in the autumn and spring. During the winter months the prevailing westerly winds drive in the ocean rollers, which throw up great columns of spray as they assault the headlands. Beneath the cliffs there are a number of inaccessible beaches where grey seals give birth to their pups in the autumn months.

Among the most familiar bird sounds to be heard along the coast are the raucous cries of herring gulls as they wheel and soar above the cliff tops or gather in noisy, quarrelsome ranks on the rocks below. On the cliff coasts look out for fulmars, shags and buzzards. With luck you may spot a peregrine falcon, a group of cliff-nesting house martins, or even a family of choughs. Dolphins and porpoises roll in the bay and seals can frequently be seen in the water close inshore beneath the cliffs. The sheltered estuary of the Afon Nyfer is particularly rich in bird life during the winter months when many species of ducks, waders and other water fowl feed on the inter-tidal mudflats. Inland in the wooded valleys those who have patience are often rewarded with sightings of badgers, wild mink, stoats, weasels and foxes. On the river banks there are otters, and hares are sometimes seen on the open farmlands.

In the spring and summer one of the glories of the Carningli area is the kaleidoscope of flowers in bloom. The stone hedgebanks along the pathways are ablaze with flowers from March to May, including snowdrops, primroses, celandines, stitchworts, dog violets and early purple orchids. Later, in the early summer, foxgloves, red campions and harebells come into their own. Woodland floors are carpeted with wood sorrel, wood anemone, wild garlic, bluebell and moschatel. High banked lanes hang with broom, mayflower and honeysuckle. The open moorlands are painted purple and gold with heather and gorse. The clifftops support cushions of thrift, vernal squill and sea campion. Sundew and butterwort, bog bean and cotton grass grow on the moorland bogs. For more information contact the Dyfed Wildlife Trust on 01437 765462.

Peregrine

CARNINGLI WALKS

The routes that have been devised for this booklet have been chosen specifically for those who enjoy walking in quiet, unspoilt, beautiful and varied countryside. The 66 km of routes described in these pages represent but a small proportion of the many walks that can be enjoyed within this compact area.

The selected routes have been chosen so as to link the wild sea coast with the high heathlands and rocky crags, taking the walker through a varied agricultural landscape and along shaded river valleys.

Each route is complete in itself, and some very popular stretches of footpath are included in more than one route description. All of the routes are discreetly waymarked by signs made of local oak and installed with the co-operation of the NPA. Some of the walks are circular; one involves a figure-of-eight route; and others take the walker to a finishing point some kilometres distant from the starting point so that return transport will need to be organised. In some cases it is possible to link routes together, or to take short cuts back to the starting point in case of bad weather. Linking routes and short cuts are mentioned in the following text and short cuts are shown on the route maps.

All of the starting points for the routes are at convenient car-parking locations. The route network is built up from a series of key locations which are identified by the letters A to N on the accompanying diagram. The diagram also shows the distances between the key points. In appropriate places fingerposts have been installed which indicate a choice of routes and give both the distances in kilometres and the timings for the average walker. There are occasional hostelries en route for those who enjoy leisurely lunches; these are mentioned, where appropriate, in the text. There are also a number of picnic sites and other locations where seats and tables are provided for the convenience of walkers.

The relics left by the Iron Age and other people who have inhabited this area, and the very beautiful countryside, have made this a "land of enchantment" which is ideal for a walking holiday. The warmth and friendliness of the local people is an added bonus! The equable climate of the area means that it is possible to enjoy the Carningli Walks at any time of year. Among the best times for walking are the early spring and late autumn, though many people believe that visitors in May and June will see the countryside at its most glorious.

Apart from the routes described in this booklet, the area has much more to offer the truly ambitious walker. It is possible to strike out along quite challenging sections of the Pembrokeshire Coast Path, both to the north-east and west of Newport; and longer ridge walks can take in either the Carningli to Dinas upland or the "Golden Road" route along the Preseli mountain ridge eastwards towards Crymych. It is also possible to walk from Newport along the whole length of the Gwaun Valley to Fishguard using quiet country roads and (at the western end) riverside and woodland paths.

Most of the walks described in the following pages are perfectly safe for those who take adequate precautions and who are well shod and well clothed. But it should always be remembered that the weather can change quite rapidly in this area, and that exposure and wind chill can affect walkers at any time outside the main holiday months. It is always a good idea to wear either walking boots or stout shoes, since many of the inland footpath sections can be muddy and even flooded after heavy rain! If possible carry waterproof clothing with you, and something to eat or drink. On the Coast Path, which provides the walker with such wonderful panoramic views, particular care should be taken since many sections of the path are right at the cliff edge. Other sections of the Coast Path can be wet and slippery, and mud slides and rock falls can damage the footpath, particularly during the winter months. The NPA tries to maintain the footpath and the coastal stiles in good condition, but nobody wants "over-management", and the walker must always recognise that there are certain dangers attached to walking in this type of terrain.

The visitor to the Carningli area should experience few difficulties with regard to accommodation and transport. There are many local self-catering cottages which can be booked throughout the year. While there are no large hotels in the area, there are several excellent guest-houses and "country farmhouse hotels" in and around Newport and close to parts of the routes described in this booklet. Some of them have many years of experience in catering for the needs of soggy ramblers and tired long-distance Coast Path walkers! There are numerous bed and breakfast establishments, although not all of them are open during the winter. A new YHA hostel is due to open on the site of the Old Primary School in 1995-96. The public transport system provides adequate bus transport on the A487 road, providing many opportunities for the walker to start or finish walks at the road/walking route intersection points. Buses pass between Fishguard and Cardigan in each direction with a frequency of almost one per hour throughout the day; check the Richards Bros timetable for precise timings. There are no bus services to Moylgrove or Cilgwyn and the Gwaun Valley; but for those who do not have cars of their own a local taxi service is available.

Walkers of all ages and abilities are welcome in the area, and are free to experience the pleasures of walking on the coast and in the countryside around Carningli. The delight of a short walking holiday can be yours simply by picking up the telephone or writing to arrange accommodation from the lists provided by the local Chamber of Trade and Tourism and by Preseli Pembrokeshire District Council. The most important points of contact are the following:

Tourism Unit, Preseli Pembrokeshire District Council, Cambria House, Haverfordwest, Pembs. SA61 1TP. Tel: 01437 – 766774. Fax: 01437 – 764382.

National Park Information Centre, Bank Cottages, Long Street, Newport, Pembs. SA42 OTN. Tel: 01239 – 820912 (Easter -September only).

Newport and District Chamber of Trade and Tourism, c/o Post Office, Newport, Pembs SA42 OTJ.

If you come to enjoy the Carningli Walks you must be prepared to fall under the spell of this "land of mystery and enchantment". Croeso!

KEY DIAGRAM
TO ROUTES

Distances are in kilometres

KEY POINTS

A Newport

B Nevern

C Treriffith

D Moylgrove

E Felindre Farchog

F Castell Henllys

G Pantry

H Parcau Field

I Penrhiw

J Sychbant

K Bedd Morris

L Aberfforest

M Aberrhigian

N Ffordd Bedd Morris

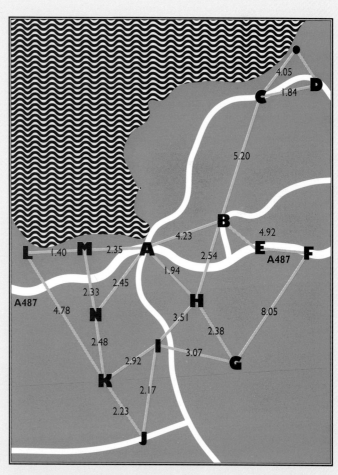

7

MOYLGROVE · NEVERN · CASTELL HENLLYS

TREWYDDEL · NANHYFER· CASTELL HENLLYS

DISTANCE
14.2 KM (8.8 MILES).

TIME
5 HRS WITHOUT STOPS.

DIFFICULTY
MODERATE.

PLACES OF INTEREST
WITCHES' CAULDRON, NEVERN CASTLE, NEVERN CHURCH, THE COLLEGE (FELINDRE FARCHOG), CASTELL HENLLYS.

PARKING
CAR PARKS AT MOYLGROVE AND NEAR CASTELL HENLLYS (A487 LAYBY), ROADSIDE PARKING AT CEIBWR AND NEVERN.

TRANSPORT
BUS TRANSPORT ON A487 AT TEMPLE BAR (NEAR NEVERN) AND AT CASTELL HENLLYS MINOR ROAD EXIT.

MAPS
OS 1:50,000 LANDRANGER SERIES SHEET 145; OS 1:25,000 PATHFINDER SERIES SHEETS 1033 AND 1010.

From **Moylgrove (D)**, past **Treriffith (C)** and on to the delightful village of **Nevern (B)**, this route takes in a section of the rugged coastline, a wooded valley, and a varied agricultural landscape. From Nevern the route follows a path through a wooded nature reserve alongside the River Nevern to Felindre Farchog(E), and thence along a beautiful minor road overlooking the Duad (a tributary of the River Nevern) to the restored Iron Age fort of Castell Henllys (F). Because the starting and finishing points of this route are widely separated, it will be necessary to organise vehicular transport from the roadside car park near Castell Henllys. Alternatively bus transport is available on the A487 road. On reaching Nevern the walker who does not wish to continue to Castell Henllys has a number of options; these are mentioned at the end of the walking instructions.

DIRECTIONS

D 1. Begin at Moylgrove car park (D). Note that there is no pub or shop in the village. Walk uphill for 30m, then turn right after Bethel Chapel towards Ceibwr. This quiet road runs above Cwm Trewyddel and after1.5 km overlooks Ceibwr beach.

2. Follow road round knoll to a grassy plateau at the coast. *From here you can see many classic structures in the cliffs; the folds and faults were created during the Caledonian mountain-building period about 400 million years ago. Photographs taken from this point have been used in many geological text-books.*

GRADIENT PROFILE

HEIGHT IN METRES ABOVE SEA LEVEL

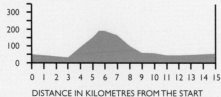

DISTANCE IN KILOMETRES FROM THE START

3. Continue uphill on the road for c 100 m, then climb over stile on right to join Pembrokeshire Coast Path. The cliff edges are

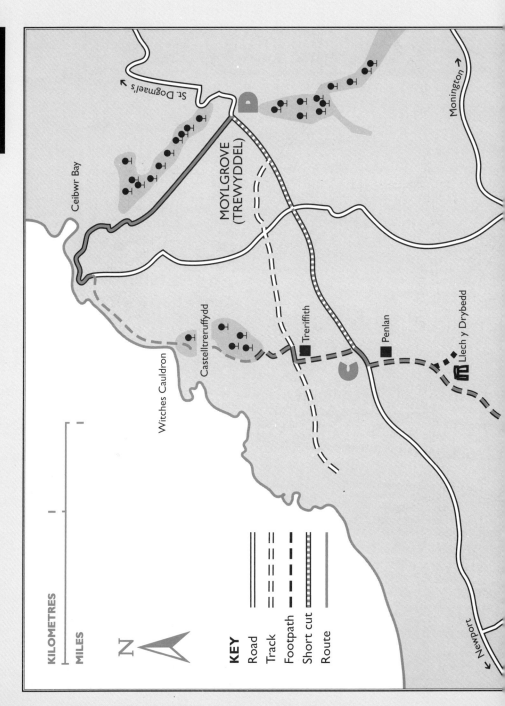

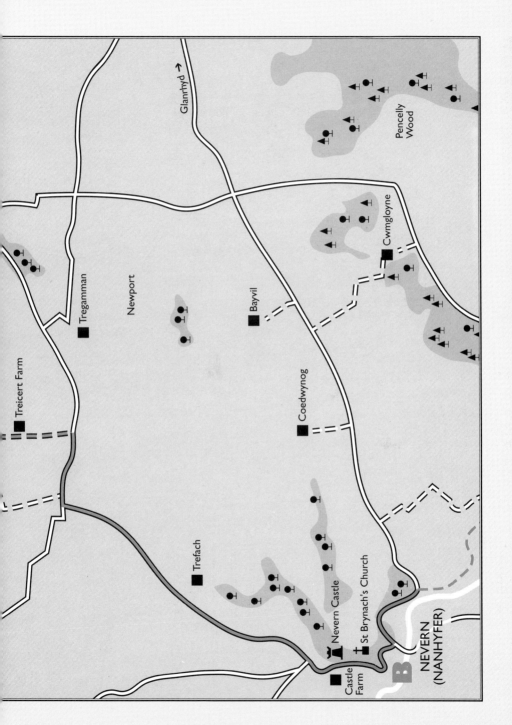

Glanrhyd →

Pencelly
Wood

Cwmgloyne

Newport

Tregamman

Bayvil

Treicert Farm

Coedwynog

Trefach

Nevern Castle

St Brynach's Church

Castle
Farm

NEVERN
(NANHYFER)

B

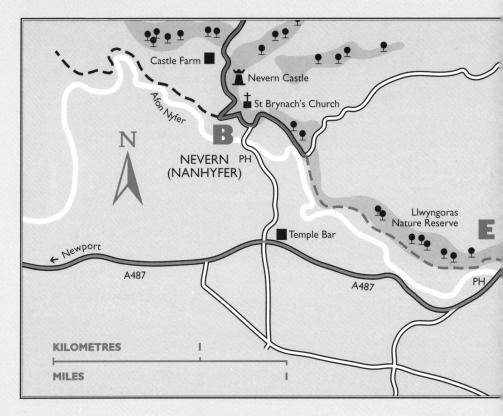

dangerous, so keep to the path. *Sea-birds abound; in particular, you should see many fulmars since there is an expanding colony on the cliffs. There is also a colony of house martins.*

4. After 1 km the path reaches the Witches Cauldron, a gigantic amphitheatre caused by the collapse of a cave roof. You cross a natural arch as you follow steps down. Keep to the path. Seals are often seen in the cauldron. At sea-level tunnels in the rocks "blow" furiously at critical tidal conditions, particularly in stormy weather. Cross concrete span. Climb up the slope, which is very steep in places. You may encounter clifftop subsidence on or adjacent to the path; keep to any marked diversions.

5. At top ridge turn left before stile, keeping barbed-wire fence to your right. After ruins of cottage near Castelltreruffydd, pass above a deep forested valley, ablaze with bluebells in springtime. Climb over stile, turn left to follow farm track uphill. (Here it can be very wet and boggy.)

6. Approach Treriffith Farm through gate. Immediately turn right to stile adjacent to farm gate. Follow track for 200 m, and turn left uphill.

Celtic Cross, Nevern.

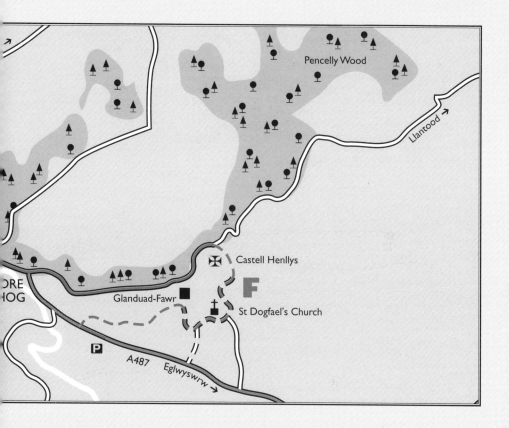

7. At stile meet Moylgrove to Newport road. (For a short circular walk turn left and follow road back to Moylgrove car park). Turn right and continue for 150 m, then turn left up farm track to Penlan.

8. Leaving farm on your left continue to crest of hill. This is Nell's Lane. At crest, Carningli ("the Mount of Angels") will come into view as will the sweep eastwards of the Preseli Hills. (Turn left at the fork for short diversion of 250 m to the Llech y Drybedd cromlech. *Like the other local cromlechs, it has a massive capstone supported by upright pillars. In Neolithic times it was covered by an elongated mound of earth and stones; the mound has long since been stripped away by grave robbers and by the forces of nature.* It is approached via a stile in hedge on right). Otherwise take the right fork and follow Nell's Lane directly to Treicert farm.

9. At farm entrance note tree on hedge ahead, and exit by lane to right of tree. On reaching metalled road, turn right and continue for 500 m.

10. At junction turn left for Nevern. Walk along the road. After c 2 km pass Castle Farm on right and continue for 200 m to Nevern Castle entrance on your left. Explore if you have time. Otherwise, view remains of castle ramparts on left as you continue along road. **The castle was built around 1110 by the Normans, in the classic "motte and bailey" style. It is an earlier and more primitive structure than Newport Castle. The castle mound is still prominent, and there are traces of masonry walls on top. The stronghold was severely damaged on a number of occasions by the Welsh princes, and it was abandoned after only about 100 years of use.**

11. Via two hair-pin bends you descend into Nevern. At the second bend, path to Newport goes off to right. (Take this path for 50 m to see Pilgrim's Cross, cut out of rock on the right). Otherwise, follow road to T- junction in Nevern. If you need liquid rather than spiritual refreshment, turn right to cross bridge for Trewern Arms. If you want to abandon the walk here and return by bus to Newport, walk past the Trewern Arms and continue to the A487 at Temple Bar. Otherwise, turn left for St. Brynach's Church with its Celtic Cross and "bleeding yews". Note the old mounting block at the roadside. Explore the church and churchyard if you have time.

B 12. From the church gate walk up the road, leaving the built-up area of the village. Continue on road for c 300m, passing picnic table on right.

13. After house on left, turn right onto track that runs parallel to road. Cross stream, then keep right. The path now follows the southern edge of the Llwyngoras Nature Reserve, managed by the Dyfed Wildlife Trust. Path can be very muddy and liable to severe flooding in winter.

14. Path joins concrete road to treatment works on right. Continue on road through Salutation Inn car park at Felindre Farchog (which means "Knights Mill-Town"). The inn is a convenient stopping place for refreshments.

E 15. Turn left onto A487 (Newport to Cardigan road) follow road for about 500 m until you come to a house on right hand side. Here turn left onto minor road. (NB: no footpath on A487, so to minimise risk please face oncoming traffic).

16. Follow this quiet rural road. After 1 km road climbs steeply. Once over the brow, descend for 100 m, and look for stile on right. After crossing stile, turn left and follow path. You are now at Castell Henllys, an Iron Age fort owned by the NPA.

F 17. Pass picnic site on left. At path T junction turn left, over bridge to follow road; pass Visitor Centre on left and Education Centre on right. If you want to visit the hillfort, tickets can be obtained from the Visitor Centre. Continue to T junction and turn right; after 100 m you reach the entrance to St Dogfael's

CEIBWR BAY

The little creek of Ceibwr is the only safe landing place on the steep and dangerous coast between Newport and the Teifi Estuary. It was used as the port for Moylgrove, and small sailing vessels beached here, bringing in cargoes of coal, limestone, timber, foodstuffs, fabrics, salt, wine and many of the other items needed by the farming community. There were also exports of wool, woollen cloth, grain, and other agricultural surpluses. There was never a landing quay, but evidence of the old coastal trade can be seen in the ruined lime kiln on the shore. This was one of the favourite places of the writer and broadcaster Wynford Vaughan-Thomas, and he presented his land on the west side of the creek to the National Trust for the enjoyment of the public.

Ceibwr Bay.

Llech y Drybedd, Burial Chamber.

Church and car park. Continue up the farm lane (not the tarmac road) and then turn right for Glanduad-Fawr. Before farm turn left and follow signposted path across fields. On reaching main road (A487) turn left and cross over to car parking area and layby on other side. If you wish to return to Newport or Cardigan by bus, you may do so from here. Carry a bus timetable with you!

LINKING ROUTES

1. Moylgrove-Newport-Moylgrove Circular Route.
Follow the minor road from Moylgrove (D) to the Treriffith farm track entrance (C). Then follow walk instructions 7-11 to the hill descent into Nevern. Turn right on the path towards Newport, passing Pilgrim's Cross. Now follow Route Five (in reverse) back towards Newport via Berry Hill Farm. On reaching the estuary of the Afon Nyfer, do not cross the iron bridge but turn right along the Coast Path towards the coast. On reaching Newport Sands (Traeth Mawr) bear right and follow the Coast Path northwards. From here, a strenuous walk of about 10 km will take you back to Ceibwr. Follow the road back to the car park in Moylgrove.

2. Moylgrove-Newport.
Follow walk instructions 1-11. From this point on disregard the signposts and obey the following instructions! Turn right at the T-junction in Nevern (B), cross the bridge and turn right onto footpath before reaching the Trewern Arms. Now follow Route Three instructions 1-3. At point (H) turn right and follow Route Six instructions 3-6 to arrive in the centre of Newport.

CASTELL HENLLYS
This is a fascinating Iron Age fort built on a spur above the Afon Duad. The work of excavating the site has gone on over many years, and was initiated by the past owner Hugh Foster. Hugh also embarked upon the reconstruction of the thatched round houses on the site, and opened it to the public. Following his death the NPA purchased Castell Henllys in 1991, and there has been a great deal of recent development culminating in the building of the new Education Centre. Archaeological work is continuing. There are now excellent displays here concerning the Iron Age in Pembrokeshire. This fort was by no means unique; tall thatched round-houses could only be built in sheltered locations, but there are hundreds of Iron Age hillforts and promontory forts all over Pembrokeshire.

NEVERN · CASTELL HENLLYS · PENTRE IFAN · NEVERN

NANHYFER · CASTELL HENLLYS · PENTRE IFAN · NANHYFER

DISTANCE
17.2 KM (10.7 MILES).

TIME
6 HRS WITHOUT BREAKS.

DIFFICULTY
MODERATE.

PLACES OF INTEREST
NEVERN CHURCH, CASTELL HENLLYS, PENTRE IFAN, TYCANOL WOODS, CWM CLYDACH.

PARKING
CAR PARK AT ROADSIDE LAYBY NEAR CASTELL HENLLYS, ROADSIDE PARKING AT NEVERN, PENTRE IFAN, CILGWYN AND PONT CLYDACH.

TRANSPORT
BUS TRANSPORT ON A487 AT LLWYNGWAIR LODGE, TEMPLE BAR (NEAR NEVERN) AND AT CASTELL HENLLYS MINOR ROAD EXIT.

MAPS
OS 1:50,000 LANDRANGER SERIES SHEET 145; OS 1:25,000 PATHFINDER SERIES SHEET 1033.

A quite delightful circular inland route combining an exploration of the Afon Nyfer, and its tributaries the Duad, Brynberian and Clydach, with two woodland nature reserves and several sites of historical importance. This route is wet and muddy in parts, especially from autumn through to late spring, so appropriate footwear is essential. The route is the longest one in this booklet, but it can be shortened by arranging return transport at one of the following points: roadside layby near **Castell Henllys (F)**, **Pentre Ifan Cromlech, Cilgwyn**.

There are also two easy routes on quiet country roads which can be used to shorten the walk back to **Nevern (B)**. Linking routes are described at the end of the walk instructions. The route crosses the **A487** at two points, giving access to the **Fishguard-Cardigan bus service**.

DIRECTIONS

B   Cars may be parked where convenient on roadside in Nevern Village (B), but please avoid parking at church entrance. Follow walking instructions 12-17 (points B – F) from Route One. Then proceed as follows:

F   1. At St. Dogfael's Church proceed straight ahead on the track (NB: do not take the tarmac drive) and at the track into Glanduad Fawr Farm turn left and then via a cattle grid up to the A487.

GRADIENT PROFILE

HEIGHT IN METRES ABOVE SEA LEVEL

DISTANCE IN KILOMETRES FROM THE START

Resconstructed Iron Age buildings at Castell Henllys.

2. Taking great care, cross over the A487 into a farm drive leading towards Pen-y-Benglog Farm. (NB: turn right along main road and walk on the grass verge if you wish to return directly to Felindre Farchog and Nevern. You can also catch local buses at this point). Just before the farm at a sharp bend follow left hand track away from the farm.

3. In about 300 m, just after a left hand bend, turn sharp right downhill. The track downhill passes one of a series of old hill fortifications hereabouts. This is Castell Llwyd. Descend via a muddy track to the road by a bridge over the Afon Nyfer. (If you want to shorten the walk at this point, turn right and follow the quiet country road for about 3 km to Sychpant Cross, where you turn right to return to Nevern.)

4. Walking on the road, proceed straight up the hill to the left. After about 100 m you cross a stile on the right. This leads to a path which crosses several fields until it eventually reaches the Afon Brynberian (another tributary of the Nyfer) through steeply wooded slopes and along quiet water meadows. Again the path can be very wet in parts.

5. Emerging onto the road by a ford, cross the river via the footbridge and walk up the road for over 1 km, passing two farm access tracks. Take the first road on the right, at Maes-y-Beddau, and in about 300 m, just past a house, turn left into a field through a gate. Follow waymarks across several fields until a road is reached.

6. At the road a small deviation of 100 m to the right leads to the well sign-posted path to Pentre Ifan cromlech. *This is the most magnificent of the local Neolithic burial chambers. The cromlech which we see today is about 4,500 years old, and it was once the core of an oval burial mound; the outlines of the mound can still be traced. Thousands of visitors come here each year to marvel at the size of the capstone and the "megalithic" skills of the Stone Age builders.* (There is a car parking area on the roadside; if you use it, lock your car securely. Return transport can be arranged here if you do not wish to complete the second part of the circular walk.)

7. Returning to the route, continue up the road until the road turns sharp left. Turn right into drive to Tycanol Farm (marked "Private Road").

Footbridge over Clydach.

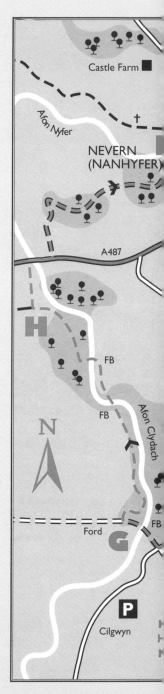

8. At farm house, follow waymarks around farm into Tycanol Woods. *The woodland is a National Nature Reserve, with ancient woodland and rock outcrops festooned with over 350 different kinds of lichens. You are welcome to enjoy the reserve by using the marked paths. Please help to protect the reserve by not climbing on rocks or trees, not collecting plants and pieces of wood and not camping or lighting fires.* Turn right at way-marked path junction in woods.

9. Follow path down through woods to stile at reserve entrance on left. On leaving the woods follow way-marks around the back of Fachongle Uchaf Farm and then down drive to Constantinople. Here you may turn right if you wish to return directly to Nevern. Otherwise turn left and proceed to a cross-

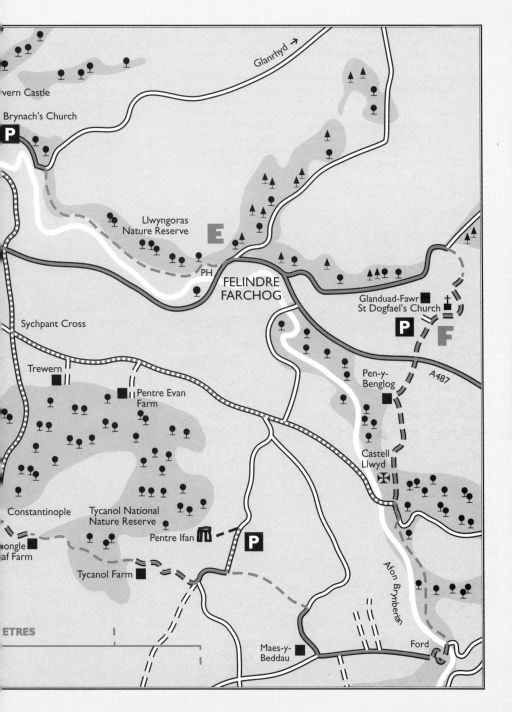

vern Castle

Brynach's Church

P

Glanrhyd →

Llwyngoras
Nature Reserve

E

PH

FELINDRE
FARCHOG

Glanduad-Fawr
St Dogfael's Church

P

F

A487

Sychpant Cross

Trewern

Pentre Evan
Farm

Pen-y-
Benglog

Castell
Llwyd

Constantinople

Tycanol National
Nature Reserve

Pentre Ifan

P

ongle
af Farm

Tycanol Farm

Afon Brynberian

ETRES

Maes-y-
Beddau

Ford

19

roads. If you wish to end your walk near here, go straight over the cross-roads and continue towards Cilgwyn, where there are a number of car-parking possibilities for return transport.

10. To continue your walk, turn right at cross-roads and go down a poorly surfaced lane to a ford. Cross the ford by the footbridge and in about 100m look for sign post and stile over wall on the right.

G 11. Cross the wall and a small field to muddy track, then over the ladder stile into field. Cross field into woods (watch for waymarks). You are now following the valley of the Afon Clydach down towards its confluence with the Nyfer. (Note: keep to way-marked paths well above the riverside areas on right, where the boggy ground can be very treacherous).

12. Eventually the path is sign-posted through the woods to a footbridge over the Afon Clydach. Cross the footbridge and head uphill for about 25m to a small gate. Go through the gate and follow the path along the top of a steep slope. Then descend to valley floor and through trees to a second footbridge opposite Allt Clydach Farm.

13. Cross the footbridge and head straight for the farm buildings. Just prior to the farm turn right onto the farm drive. In about 300 m where the drive turns sharp left at cross-tracks, keep straight on, ignoring track down to right. Follow a narrow path then a track around to a sign post (H). The track can be very wet and muddy.

H 14. At the sign-post turn right into field. Pass the standing stone and keep to right hand side of field to bottom right hand corner. Cross stile and descend steep slope to A487. Note: take care, since the slope can be slippery.

ST BRYNACH
The founder of Nevern Church (and the monastery which is now lost without trace) was an Irishman named Brynach, who was a contemporary and close friend of St David. As a young nobleman he lived a somewhat wild life and travelled widely, but after his conversion he settled in north Pembrokeshire. The Gwaun Valley was not to his liking, and legend tells how he was led from Pontfaen to found his monastery near the spot where the church now stands. In the local area he was greatly revered for his good works, and the Church is dedicated to him. The tall Celtic Cross in the churchyard is also referred to locally as "St Brynach's Cross." Brynach loved Carningli, and often retired there to commune with the angels.

Newport Bay seen from the flank of Carningli.

15. Turn right and cross road (BEWARE fast moving traffic) and proceed to Llwyngwair Lodge (the circular gate-house of Llwyngwair Manor) in about 150 m. Buses will stop here for Cardigan or Newport. Just beyond gate-house turn left along drive, to right of caravan park.

16. In about 300 m watch for sharp turning on right just before derelict barns and stables. Follow this wide track through old woodland, carpeted with bluebells in the spring, until you encounter three gates ahead.

17. Take the middle gate and walk along a narrow lane (referred to by the locals as "Sandy Lane") and through woods before eventually crossing a field towards Nevern Bridge, near the Trewern Arms. Cross stile and turn left at the road with the inn nearby, and cross the bridge to complete your walk.

B

Ancient oak tree in Tycanol Woods.

TYCANOL NATURE RESERVE

The woodland at Tycanol is a magical place, but it is also very important scientifically. In particular it is famous for the huge variety of lichens which inhabit its trees and rock surfaces; many of the lichens are indicators of air quality, and the wood is full of test sites where botanical observations are made on a regular basis. The gnarled oak trees twist and creep in and out of rock crevices. There are tors, caves and boulders of volcanic rock especially at the western end of the wood, and the highest spur to the south of the footpath was used as a defended settlement site by an Iron Age tribal group. According to a local legend, the oak groves were used by the Druids for pagan ceremonies prior to the adoption of Christianity. The reserve is owned by the NPA and managed by the Countryside Council for Wales; additional information is provided on display panels at the reserve entry/exit points.

LINKING ROUTES

1. Nevern-Cilgwyn-Sychbant (Cwm Gwaun). This is a pleasant one-way walk using public roads and some sections of marked footpath. Walk due south from Nevern on the minor road via Temple Bar, Sychpant Cross and Constantinople. Continue to cross-roads, turn right and descend to ford. Cross ford and continue up lane to Cilgwyn Road. Turn left and follow Route Three instructions 10-14 through to Sychbant car park and picnic site.

2. Nevern-Cilgwyn-Newport. Follow instructions in above paragraph to Cilgwyn Road. Turn right, and then left up track just before Bryn Aeron. Go through gate, and bear right across moorland, climbing up to Dolrannog Road. From car parking area walk up green track (old tramway route) towards Carningli until you cross a well-used north-south track. Turn right along Route Five route and follow it (in reverse) back to Newport.

Pentre Ifan Cromlech.

NEVERN · CLYDACH VALLEY · SYCHBANT

NANHYFER · CWM CLYDACH · SYCHBANT

DISTANCE
11.3 KM (7 MILES).

TIME
4 HRS WITHOUT STOPS.

DIFFICULTY
STRENUOUS IN PART.

PLACES OF INTEREST
NEVERN CHURCH, CWM CLYDACH, CILGWYN CANDLES MUSEUM, PENLAN UCHAF GARDENS.

PARKING
CAR PARKS AT PONT CLYDACH (LAY-BY), SYCHBANT. ROADSIDE PARKING AT NEVERN.

TRANSPORT
BUS TRANSPORT ON A487 AT LLWYNGWAIR LODGE.

MAPS
OS 1:50,000 LANDRANGER SERIES SHEET 145; OS 1:25,000 PATHFINDER SERIES SHEET 1033.

Starting at Nevern (B), this is a lovely route including the secret and well-wooded valley of Cwm Clydach, and finishing with a descent of the deciduous woods in the eastern Gwaun Valley. The paths can be wet and muddy in places, with some steep climbs as well, so please wear suitable footwear. This is a one-way route, so if you wish to follow it all the way transport will have to be arranged at Sychbant (J). There are no short cuts, but a number of "linking options" are described at the end of the walking instructions. There is only one bus stopping place on the route, at Llwyngwair Lodge on the A487.

DIRECTIONS

B 1. Starting from Nevern Church walk across the bridge towards the Trewern Arms. Immediately after bridge, cross stile by gate on your right. Follow the track across field until you reach a gate leading into the woods.

2. Cross stile and follow track though woods, then continue along "Sandy Lane" to gate before next woods. Go through gate and keep straight ahead on woodland track. Cross stone stile and descend to driveway. Nearby is the Llwyngwair Manor Hotel, where refreshments are available. Turn sharp left and follow the drive until you reach the A487 road at Llwyngwair Lodge. Cardigan-Fishguard buses will stop here if asked. Turn right and cross bridge. (If you want to take a short cut back to Newport at this point, simply follow the main road westwards. But beware of speeding traffic).

3. From lay-by on the other side of the road ascend rough stone steps and climb path through trees to stile. Take care – the path can be slippery. Cross stile and proceed straight ahead along

GRADIENT PROFILE

HEIGHT IN METRES ABOVE SEA LEVEL

300
200
100
0

0 1 2 3 4 5 6 7 8 9 10 11 12

DISTANCE IN KILOMETRES FROM THE START

edge of field to join farm track. Follow track along edge of field, to gate at top. Note the standing stone on your right.

H 4. Turn left after gate and follow track into woods above Cwm Clydach. *The valley was home to several water mills in the 18th-19th century, mostly used for the milling of corn and "furze" or gorse. It is now a deserted "secret" valley, a paradise for wildlife.* Continue along path to junction with farm tracks.

Nevern Church.

5. Turn left on main track down hill (second turning on left), and proceed down track to old farm (Allt Clydach). Turn left before farm, and cross rough pasture to footbridge..Cross footbridge and turn half-right to follow track uphill to crest of slope.

6. Follow crest to small gate, then veer right downhill, reaching second footbridge after about 25 m.

7. After crossing footbridge at Gamallt turn half-left and head up through wood (about 40 m) to fingerpost above woodline. Follow path uphill, then downhill through woods, to cross three brooks. Keep well above wet areas on left, which can be dangerous.

Llwyngwair Lodge.

8. Emerge from woods into field at junction of old boundarywalls, and cross field towards wooden ladder stile to right of clump of trees. Cross stile and follow muddy lane and small field to next stile.

G 9. Cross stile, and turn right to follow rough lane up to its junction with the Newport-Cilgwyn road. You have three options here. If you want to complete a shorter walk returning to Newport, turn right and follow the Cilgwyn Road all the way back to the town (2.4 km). If you want to arrange return transport to Nevern, use the parking area on the Dolrannog Road. To reach it, turn right and after 200 m take track up to left, just before Bryn Aeron. Go through gate, and on reaching open moorland walk uphill to the metalled road. Turn right to car-parking area at roadside.

10. Those who wish to continue to Cwm Gwaun should turn left and follow road downhill for about 450 m, passing Trefelin and Cilgwyn Candle Museum and Workshop. *The making of rushlights and hand-dipped taper candles was once a part of the annual domestic routine in local cottages and farms. The raw material for candle-making was tallow, rendered down from various animal fats. Now paraffin wax is used, together with various scents and dyes. This is the only place in Wales where hand-dipped candles are still made on a commercial scale.* Cross bridge over Afon Clydach and follow road uphill, keeping right at road junction. Continue to the T-junction at Tyriet farmhouse. (Here there are bicycles for hire.)

11. Turn right and follow road towards Cwm Gwaun for about 450 m until Banc-y-Rhyd is reached on the left. (On the way, you pass Penfeidr Cwm, where cream teas are sometimes available.) Opposite Banc-y-Rhyd, turn right onto track at gate, and continue along track for short distance. After disused pig sties, turn left over stile. Follow way-marked path uphill, veering right into wood.

12. At entrance to wood, proceed straight ahead up the steep slope, following the yellow way-mark posts to stile at top. Cross stile, and follow path along edge of wood by fence, crossing stiles and stream before veering right to arrive at Penrhiw Farm. Cross farm entrance and turn left along the farm track.

I 13. On reaching Penrhiw Fach (not marked on the map), keep straight on along green lane down to Llannerch Farm. The first section of the track can be very muddy in wet weather, but can be by-passed with care along hedge banks. Follow track down through woods, passing through two gates.

14. On reaching Llannerch Farm, pass through gate into farmyard and follow concrete drive down to road. Turn right and follow the Cwm Gwaun road. *If you have time, visit the Penlan Uchaf Gardens, which are ablaze with colour in the summer and which provide glorious views over Cwm Gwaun; see sign on right. Refreshments are available.* Continue to Sychbant car park and picnic site. Here you can
J collect your return transport.

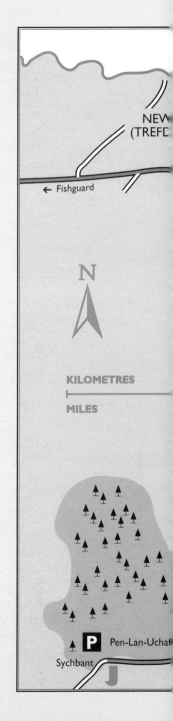

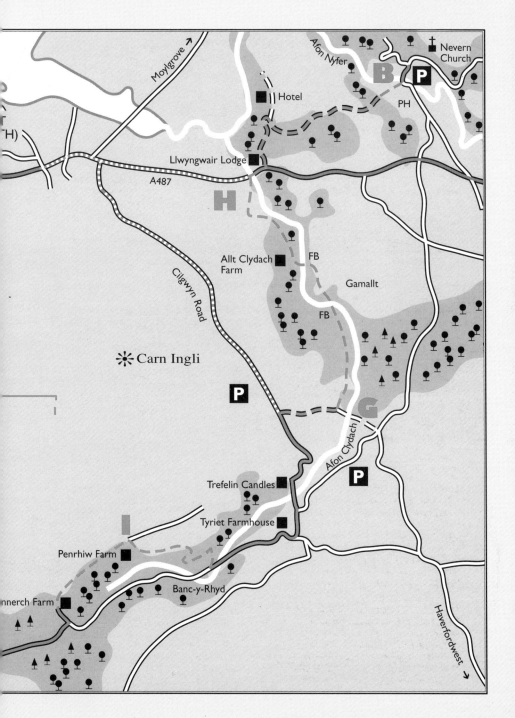

Moylgrove →

Afon Nyfer

† Nevern
Church

B

P

PH

Hotel

Llwyngwair Lodge

A487

H

(H)

Allt Clydach
Farm

FB

Gamallt

FB

☀ Carn Ingli

P

Cilgwyn Road

G

Afon Clydach

P

Trefelin Candles

Tyriet Farmhouse

I

Penrhiw Farm

nnerch Farm

Banc-y-Rhyd

Haverfordwest →

STRANGE TALES
The area around Dolrannog and Llannerch has a reputation as a somewhat spooky place, and indeed the Gwaun Valley as a whole abounds with stories of witches, phantom funerals, witchcraft and ghosts. One story from Dolrannog Isaf relates how a notoriously wicked old farmer died and was laid out in the parlour prior to the funeral. During the night a group of phantom horsemen arrived and transported the body away to Hell, leaving the family to bury a pile of stones in the coffin instead. Another story tells how a local farm worker was followed on the Penrhiw-Llannerch track by a phantom in a long black coat, with a tall black hat on his head. Convinced that he had been followed and marked out by the "Grim Reaper", the man became ill and died shortly afterwards.

Small stream, Cwm Gwaun.

LINKING ROUTES

1. Nevern-Cilgwyn-Bedd Morris-Newport. Follow walking instructions 1-9 above. But instead of turning right on Dolrannog Road, turn left. At edge of moorland turn right past ruined Carningli Lodge. From this point on you are on common land, and the route is not waymarked. Follow path to right of boundary wall, turn left at corner and continue along path all the way to Bedd Morris (K). Then follow Route Seven instructions 1-3. At point (N) turn right and follow Route Six instructions 18-22 to the centre of Newport.

2. Nevern-Sychbant-Bedd Morris-Aberfforest. At the end of the described route (and after taking a rest at Sychbant!) walk up the steep tributary valley into the woods, following Route Four waymarks in reverse. At Bedd Morris (K) walk northwards down road and then turn left and follow path across Parc Mawr. Now follow Route Seven waymarks all the way to Aberfforest.

SYCHBANT · PENRHIW · BEDD MORRIS · SYCHBANT

This pleasant circular route starts and finishes at Sychbant car park and picnic site (J) in Cwm Gwaun. Over a distance of 7.5 km (nearly 5 miles) you explore the eastern end of Cwm Gwaun, with panoramic views over to Mynydd Preseli after an ascent through oak woodland. A moorland walk is followed by a descent through thick coniferous forest. There are some steep gradients and some muddy sections, so please wear appropriate footwear. The walk can be shortened by arranging transport at Bedd Morris (K), where there is ample car parking space. There are a number of options for linking this route with others described in this booklet.

DIRECTIONS

J 1. From car park (Sychbant picnic site), turn left and walk along road for 1.5 km to Llannerch Farm. At concrete farm drive, turn left and walk towards farm. Keep left at farm house, passing through gate.

2. Veer right to pass through second gate, and follow track uphill through woods to gate at top. Pass through gate, and follow muddy track (keeping along hedge bank if necessary) to first farm (Penrhiw Fach). The farm is not marked on the map.

3. Turn left immediately after farm, to follow track up edge of field, crossing four stiles. (First section is wet and muddy). Continue along track to fifth stile. Cross stile and follow path to right of rock outcrop (Carn Edward) up to wall at edge of moorland. *Carn Edward is a tumbledown tor, very similar to the tors of Dartmoor but here made of dolerite rather than granite. The tor has been greatly eroded by over-riding glacier ice during the Ice Age, and the work of frost has also helped to detach massive blocks which have slid downhill.*

GRADIENT PROFILE

HEIGHT IN METRES ABOVE SEA LEVEL

DISTANCE IN KILOMETRES FROM THE START

4. Turn left at wall, to stile by gate which leads onto moorland. Cross stile, and turn left to follow path across moorland, keeping parallel to

---

DISTANCE
7.5 KM (ALMOST 5 MILES)

TIME
2 HRS 45 MINS WITHOUT STOPS.

DIFFICULTY
MODERATE.

PLACES OF INTEREST
PENLAN UCHAF GARDENS, CARN EDWARD TOR, BEDD MORRIS STANDING STONE.

PARKING
CAR PARKS AT SYCHBANT AND BEDD MORRIS.

TRANSPORT
NO BUSES NEAR THIS ROUTE.

MAPS
OS 1:50,000 LANDRANGER SERIES SHEET 145; OS 1:25,000 PATHFINDER SERIES SHEET 1033.

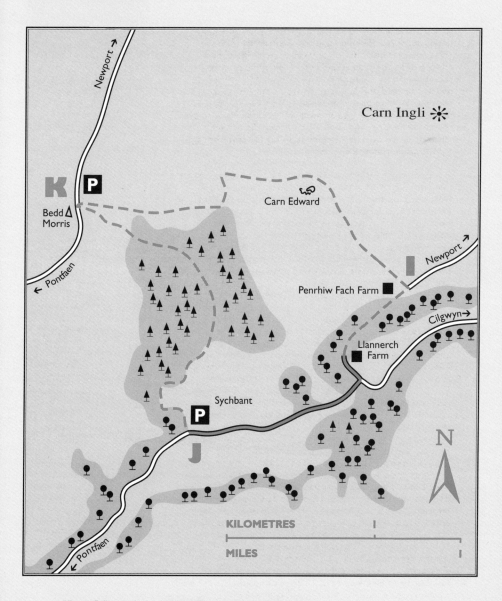

wall/fence. Follow path alongside wall/fence, to corner of fence, and turn left. Then follow path along fence to next corner, above coniferous forest. Turn right to follow path alongside fence. (NB: do not cross stile at corner into forest).

5. Follow path alongside fence to last corner, then keep on path straight across moorland towards road. (Look for standing stone by car park. NB: Sections of moorland path can be very wet and muddy).

K 6. Cross road and take a look at Bedd Morris standing stone. *Bedd Morris is a fine example of a Bronze Age standing stone, which is also a parish boundary mark. There are a number of legends concerned with it; according to one, Morris was a notorious robber who waylaid travellers here and was hanged and buried on the spot. According to another, Morris was a young man killed by a rival in a duel for the hand of the heiress of Pontfaen. Traditionally, the boys of Newport are (gently) beaten here during the annual "Beating of the Bounds" Ceremony in August, as a warning against future misdemeanours!*

7. From facing the stone, turn left towards Cwm Gwaun and follow road for short distance to signpost at cattle grid. Veer to left, through stile onto moorland. Turn left and follow path close to fence across wet area. Then veer right to join track across moorland towards forest, keeping right at path junction to follow track alongside old field boundary wall. Continue along track to stile into forest.

8. Cross stile into forest, and follow track down through trees. Keep right at path junction (left is marked to Carn Ingli). Keep on track downhill to bottom of forest, taking care over wet and muddy sections.

9. At bottom of forest, turn right to follow path alongside fence. Ignore first stile and proceed down to second stile in fence on left. Cross stile, and walk down to path junction above valley. Turn right at sign post to descend path. Cross bridge over two streams. (NB: This section of path is very rocky and wet).

10. Continue on path to cross third stream (no bridge) and proceed along to finger post (waymarked). At path junction turn left to cross wall and go on path downhill through trees. This section of path is very steep, and can be slippery.

11. Carry on down to way-marked path junction, then turn left. Note viewpoint (with seat) on hillock to right. Continue on path downhill to path junction. *The buildings straight ahead on the skyline belong to Ffald y Brenin, a Christian Retreat Centre, very sensitively converted from the old Sychbant Farm. The centre includes a circular Chapel at its northern end.*

12. At path junction (way-marked) by river, turn right to follow path downhill to Sychbant picnic site (toilets and car park). *The Gwaun Valley was formed during the last Ice Age around 200,000 years ago, when much of north Pembrokeshire was covered with a vast ice sheet. Huge volumes of melt-water flowed in tunnels within and beneath the ice, gouging out channels with steep sides (like Cwm Gwaun) that today*
J *contain much smaller rivers and streams.*

LINKING ROUTES

1. Sychbant – Bedd Morris – Parrog, via Aberrhigian.
Follow walking instructions 1-6, and at Bedd Morris (K) turn

CWM GWAUN WOODLANDS
The ancient woodlands of the Gwaun Valley have been designated an SSSI on the grounds of their outstanding ecological diversity. Some of the woods may have remained intact ever since the original settlement of this area over 6,000 years ago. Among the deciduous trees are oak, ash, beech, sycamore, holly, hazel, elder and horse chestnut. Parts of the woodland have been clear-felled or coppiced in the past, and there are coniferous plantations also, as for example in the Llannerch area. There is also a valuable area of wetland designated as a Nature Reserve; this is the Llannerch Alder Carr, on the valley floor close to the point where the Afon Gwaun flows in from a side valley. The reserve is not open to the public.

THE BRONZE AGE
There are many traces of the Bronze Age in the Carningli Walks area, and it seems that the Carningli-Dinas Mountain upland was particularly favoured as a settlement area suitable for the grazing of domesticated animals. Apart from Bedd Morris there are many other standing stones on the flanks of the upland; they may have been waymarks, memorial stones or even fertility symbols. There are small mounds on the summit ridge which are probably burial sites, and other Bronze Age features inslude hut circles, animal enclosures and stone walls. Parts of the "man-made landscape" around Carningli are thus over 4,000 years old.

Bedd Morris – a Bronze Age standing stone.

right on the road towards Newport. Follow Route Seven instructions 1-8 as far as Aberrhigian, then turn right and follow Coast Path back to Parrog and Newport.

2. Sychbant – Carningli – Newport. Follow route instructions 1-3 via Penrhiw to Carn Edward. On reaching moorland, turn right and then bear gradually left and uphill towards Carningli summit. Visit the hillfort and follow track towards Newport (several options near the summit, but beware of steep rocky slopes). Keep to track towards Carn Llwyd and then follow tracks and lanes towards College Square and Newport town centre.

3. Sychbant – Newport via Carningli Lodge. This is a bracing walk which takes you onto the flank of Mynydd Carningli and thence to Newport on the Cilgwyn Road. Follow walking instructions 1-3 above, but on reaching the moorland at Carn Edward turn right. Follow well-marked track along moorland edge to the southern corner of the mountain. Bear right and descend to ruined Carningli Lodge. Follow moorland track or Dolrannog Road northward back to Newport.

4. Sychbant – Newport via Ffordd Bedd Morris. Follow above instructions 1-6 as far as Bedd Morris. Then turn right and follow Ffordd Bedd Morris (the public road) northwards. Follow Route Seven instructions 1-3 to Point (N). Then follow Route Six instructions 18-22, eventually descending Mill Lane back to Newport.

NEWPORT · NEVERN · SYCHBANT

TREFDRAETH · NANHYFER · SYCHBANT

DISTANCE
12.5 KM (7.5 MILES).

TIME
4 HRS WITHOUT STOPS.

DIFFICULTY
MODERATE.

PLACES OF INTEREST
PARROG, NEVERN CHURCH, CARNINGLI HILLFORT, PENLAN UCHAF GARDENS.

PARKING
CAR PARKS AT PARROG, PONT CLYDACH (LAY-BY) AND SYCHBANT. ROADSIDE PARKING AT NEVERN.

TRANSPORT
BUS STOPPING PLACE ON A487 AT LLWYNGWAIR LODGE.

MAPS
OS 1:50,000 LANDRANGER SERIES SHEET 145; OS 1:25,000 PATHFINDER SERIES 1033 AND 1010.

Starting at Parrog (A), this route follows the Afon Nyfer to Nevern (B) through a picturesque wooded valley, and then climbs to open moorland below Carningli before dropping down through woodland to Cwm Gwaun. It covers a wide range of landscapes, from estuary to mountain, and provides panoramic views over the north Pembrokeshire coast and mountains. Conditions underfoot can be wet and muddy, so please wear suitable footwear. Remember to arrange return transport from the Sychbant car park (J) in Cwm Gwaun. The first part of this route can be made into a circular route similar to the "eastern circuit" of Route Six. There are two short cuts back to Newport. A longer and very beautiful circular route is described below, after the walking instructions.

DIRECTIONS

A 1. Start at the Parrog car park in Newport. Turn left to follow road for 200 m to coast path sign.

2. Turn left onto coast path and follow path alongside estuary. Immediately after first road junction look for site of old motte

GRADIENT PROFILE

HEIGHT IN METRES ABOVE SEA LEVEL

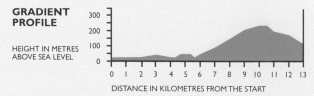

DISTANCE IN KILOMETRES FROM THE START

and bailey earthworks on right (Yr Hen Castell). Carry on to the bridge. *Note Interpretative Panel on left which pictures winter birds on the estuary. On the other side of the road (if the tide is out) you can see in the river the ancient stepping stones used by pilgrims in the Middle Ages and by local people in more recent times.*

3. Turn left and cross the "iron bridge" (scheduled for replacement). Follow road for about 1km up to Berry Hill Farm on right. Immediately after farm, turn right and cross stile for

path into woods. Follow path down to junction. Turn left at path junction and follow track down into woods, veering right at hairpin bend. The woodland floor is carpeted with bluebells in spring.

4. At bottom of hill, keep left towards cottage. Pass cottage and keep left on path to Nevern along base of woods. (Turn right at cottage if you want to take short-cut return to Newport. This route will take you over Pont Newydd and past Llwyngwair Manor on the way to the A487 road. Then turn right for Newport).

5. Continue along path, passing ruined cottage before coming to river banks of Afon Nyfer. (WARNING: path on rocks can be very wet and slippery. If flooded, scramble through woods above). Continue on path along river bank towards cottages. *Otters, mink, river fish and many species of woodland birds can be seen along this stretch of the Afon Nyfer.*

6. Immediately after cottages, cross concrete track and foot-bridge. Ascend path to metalled drive. Turn left then right, to second gate on right. Turn right into field through small side gate. Cross field, keeping on the level. Look for stile on right hand side.

7. Cross stile to follow path high above river. (WARNING: first section of path is hazardous, so take care). Continue on path to next stile. Cross stile and keep to right side of field, following path uphill to next stile.

8. Cross stile and follow path until you reach the road. *You pass a simple Pilgrim's Cross carved in a rock face near the road, with a kneeling stone below. This was used by pilgrims in Medieval times on their way to St. David's.* (If you wish to visit Nevern Castle, which was once more important than Newport Castle, turn left up the road immediately after the Pilgrim's Cross and continue to castle entrance on right. It is possible to descend from the castle site via a woodland path to Nevern Church and thence to the village.)

9. If you are not walking via the castle, turn right at road and proceed downhill to road T-junction in centre of Nevern. At junction take a short diversion (to left) to see St. Brynach's Church. *The little church, in a lovely wooded setting adjacent to a rushing stream, was founded around 570 AD by the Irish monk Brynach. Note its Norman tower, 11th century Celtic Cross and "bleeding yew trees". According to legend, the first cuckoo of spring sings on the cross on St Brynach's Day, April 7th, each year.*

B 10. From the T-junction, follow road across bridge towards Trewern Arms. Follow instructions 1-3 (B-H) from Route Three. (If you wish, you can shorten the walk when you reach Llwyngwair Lodge by following the main road directly back to Newport).

H 11. At sign-post turn right after gate and follow track for a short distance to next gate. Immediately before gate, turn left to ascend steep stone stile into field. Proceed straight ahead up edge of field. At top, cross through opening in wall, then veer right to track into woods.

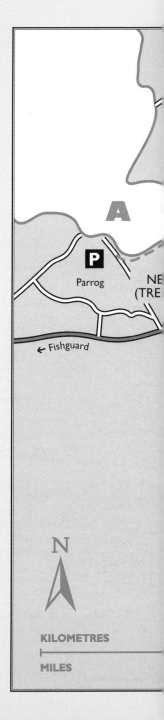

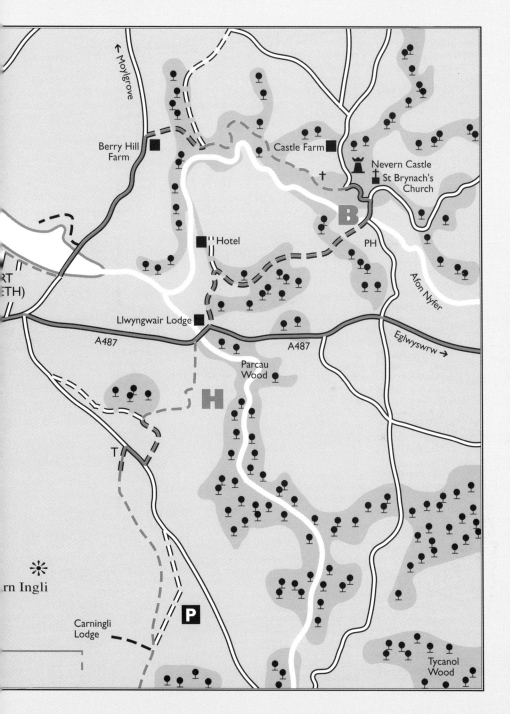

12. Follow track into woods, and after 100m bear left at signpost to ascend path crossing field towards top corner. Here you can cross high wooden stile onto track. (You can turn right here for a short cut return to Newport: 1.5 km and 20 mins. Follow lane to T-junction, turn right and walk down Greystones Hill to the town).

13. To continue way-marked walk, turn left and follow track to Newport-Cilgwyn road, veering right at track T-junction. Turn right at road towards red telephone kiosk.

14. Turn left before kiosk, and follow lane up to gate. Go through gate and proceed uphill along track to edge of moorland. Ahead of you is Mynydd Carningli (347 m). **The craggy mountain is of volcanic origin and is the site of an Early Iron Age hill fort near its summit. This is one of three "summit settlement sites" in Pembrokeshire; the others are at Foeldrygarn (near Crymych) and Garn Fawr (near Strumble Head).**

15. At top of lane, veer left to follow path running alongside wall across bottom of moorland. There are wonderful views to the left to Tycanol Woods, Carnedd Meibion Owen and Mynydd Preseli.

16. At end of wall, keep straight on along path across moorland. **You cross a tramway incline which leads up to a little mountain quarry; the track (traces of which can still be seen) carried building stones for Newport. The quarry continued in use into the 1930's, providing stone to a crushing plant for use in road-building works.** Continue along path to junction with road at edge of moorland near the ruins of Carningli Lodge. Go straight ahead at road and proceed to fourth farm. Pass entrance on right (Penrhiw Fach). Note that this farm is not marked on the map.

17. Keep straight on to follow green lane. From this point on, follow instructions 13-14 from Route Three, descending to Llannerch Farm and finishing at Sychbant car park.

THE PARROG
This was Newport's port, used for well over 1,000 years by the seafaring community of the town. The little peninsula now referred to as the Parrog was probably a natural spit of land to start with, but it has been modified greatly by the hand of man. The quays, warehouses and lime kilns were built on reclaimed land in the eighteenth century, and for more than a hundred years Parrog was a hive of activity with sailing vessels of many types calling on a regular basis. There were also a number of shipyards up-river of the port. But silting in the estuary became a problem, and by the time of the Second World War the coastal trade had died. Nowadays the Parrog is a popular base for sailing boats and other leisure craft.

CARNINGLI
Newport's little mountain rises to an altitude of only 347m, but because of its steep and rocky profile, and its proximity to the coast, it dominates a large area of countryside. It was once referred to as "Mons Angelorum", and the Welsh name may mean "Mount of Angels". It was here that St Brynach came for his periods of retreat and contemplation, and the summit still has a calm and spiritual atmosphere. Originally this was a volcanic peak, and the hard blue dolerite stone is similar to the "bluestone" of the eastern Preseli Hills. The crags and tumbled frost-shattered rocks on the south side of the summit are particularly impressive. All around we can see abundant traces of defensive walls, hut circles, animal enclosures and settlement platforms built by the Iron Age inhabitants of the mountain.

Carningli.

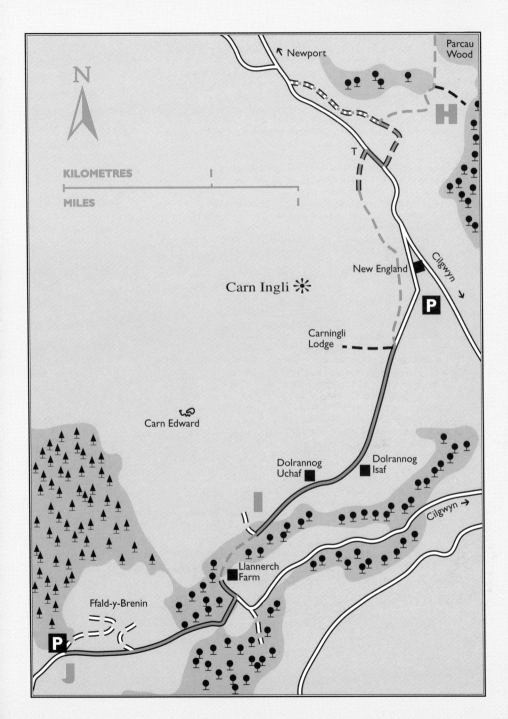

LINKING ROUTES

1. Around Cilgwyn. Starting in Newport, walk up the Cilgwyn Road as far as the red telephone kiosk. Then follow instructions 14-17 above, reaching Penrhiw Farm. Turn left before the farm. You are now on the route of Route Three, which you can follow (in reverse) to Pantry (G). Then follow Route Two instructions 11-14. Return to Newport on the A487, or on any of the other routes which present themselves.

2. Around Carningli. Start from Newport and walk to the red telephone kiosk on the Cilgwyn Road. Follow instructions 14-17 to Penrhiw Fach Farm (I). Now follow Route Four instructions 3-6 until you reach Bedd Morris (K). Turn right down road, following Route Seven instructions 1-2 as far as point (N). Turn right and follow Route Six instructions 18-22 to return to Newport.

The riverside woodland of Afon Nyfer.

NEWPORT · NEVERN · ABERRHIGIAN · NEWPORT

TREFDRAETH · NANHYFER · ABERRHIGIAN · TREFDRAETH

DISTANCE
16 KM (10 MILES).

TIME
5HRS 30 MINS. WITHOUT STOPS.

DIFFICULTY
MODERATE.

PLACES OF INTEREST
PARROG, NEVERN CHURCH, NEWPORT CASTLE AND CHURCH, SEA QUARRIES, OLD CATTLE POUND.

PARKING
CAR PARKS AT PARROG, LONG STREET (NEWPORT), PONT CLYDACH (LAY-BY) AND SYCHBANT. ROADSIDE PARKING AT NEVERN AND FFORDD BEDD MORRIS.

TRANSPORT
BUSES WILL STOP ON A487 AT PONT NEWYDD, NEWPORT TOWN CENTRE, AND LLWYNGWAIR LODGE.

MAPS
OS 1:50,000 LANDRANGER SERIES SHEET 145; OS 1:25,000 PATHFINDER SERIES 1033 AND 1010.

This is a highly varied "figure of eight" route. It involves sea-shore, salt-marsh, river-bank, rich farmland, sea cliffs, marginal hill farms and open moorland, all in a relatively compact area. There is also ample opportunity to examine the Ancient Borough of Newport (A) at the beginning of the walk, at the end, or in the middle! In the town there are four inns as well as a good range of restaurants and shops. Outside the town there are wet and muddy patches through most of the year and appropriate footwear is essential. Bus transport is available at all of the A487 intersection points on this route. Because this route is at the very heart of the network, it can be linked into all of the others in the walks series.

DIRECTIONS

A 1. Start the route from the Parrog car park. Spend a little time wandering around the old port of Newport. Note the Boat Club, the last remaining warehouse from a thriving trading past. *Note also the unusual "double lime kiln", where limestone and anthracite brought in by sea were burnt. The lime produced provided an essential dressing for the acid soils of the area.*

2. Follow Route Five instructions 1-10 (A-B) and Route Three instructions 1-3 (B-H). After crossing the A487 road you eventually reach the top corner of a field.

GRADIENT PROFILE

HEIGHT IN METRES ABOVE SEA LEVEL

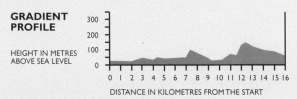

DISTANCE IN KILOMETRES FROM THE START

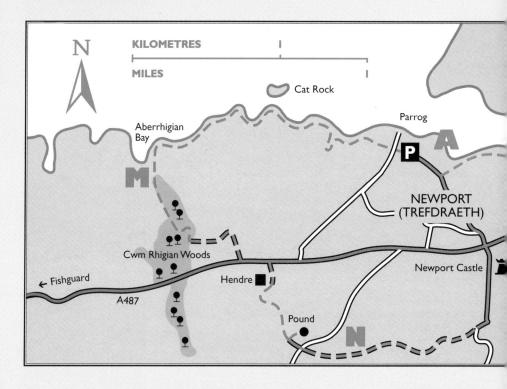

H 3. At the sign post turn right and in 50 m seek a high stile on your left. Cross the stile and climb the hill to the top right hand corner. Cross the wall and veer right along a track (NB: do not turn hard right).

4. At waymark post in 200 m, keep straight on. Veer to left of gate ahead and in 30m cross stile on the right. Descend steps to turn left through gate, and head to left of farm. Pass through gate and veer up left towards telegraph pole, to take track on right to small cottage (Brynhelig). Cross stile by house, then a kissing gate and cross several small fields and stiles to road at Greystones Farm, heading towards Newport.

5. Turn right on reaching road and in 100m continue straight ahead to College Square. Bear right to the Church, which is well worth a visit. **Newport Castle, on its castle mound to the left, is owned by the Lady Marcher of the Barony of Cemaes and cannot be visited.**

6. Keep straight on before turning right into Market Street for shops, tea-rooms, restaurants and inns. Ample opportunities for light refreshments. At cross roads proceed downhill into Long Street, and continue straight ahead past the car park and new primary school (Ysgol Bro Ingli).

NEWPORT CASTLE
The castle was built by the Norman William FitzMartin around 1191, after he had been driven from his original castle at Nevern by assorted revolting Welsh princes. It became a magnificent and imposing stone fortress with a massive gatehouse and three other towers connected by a solid curtain wall. The castle had a chequered history, and by the middle of the Sixteenth Century it was in "utter ruin". It remained so until 1859 when Sir Thomas Lloyd converted the gatehouse into a residence. Other rebuilding work followed, and it is now quite difficult to make out the features of the original fortified structure. Essential restoration work is now under way. The castle is not open to the public.

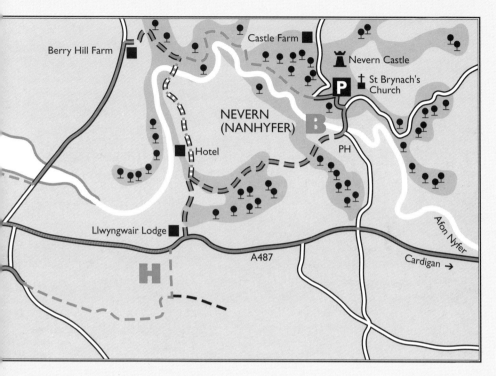

Berry Hill Farm

Castle Farm

♜ Nevern Castle

🅿 ✝ St Brynach's Church

NEVERN (NANHYFER)

B

Hotel

PH

Llwyngwair Lodge

H

A487

Cardigan →

Afon Nyfer

Unloading a sailing ship on the Parrog around 1920.

The renovated cattle pound near Ffordd Bedd Morris.

7. At the sign-post and estuary turn left and follow coast path to road. This excellent track has been upgraded by the NPA for use by disabled people. At road turn right and return to Parrog car-park.

8. Leaving Parrog car-park turn right down slip-way to foreshore. Proceed across sands to Rock House, thence to slip-way up to Bryn-y-Mor. (If the tide is in use causeway along top of sea wall, from Parrog car-park. At high tide, turn left at road before Rock House, then in 20 m turn right across field, then down steps to rejoin path at Bryn-y-Mor). The "high tide route" is well signposted!

9. Turn left up slip-way to access road in front of houses. Look back and you will get an excellent view of the Boat Club and the Afon Nyfer Estuary. Continue along surfaced trackway. **Beyond the last house note a stone building beside path with an opening onto the route; this was once a public house and has now been renovated as a cottage. On arrival at Cwm note the old lifeboat station, opened in 1884 and used only for a decade or so. Silting at the mouth of the river was such a problem that the lifeboat was moved away in 1895.**

10. On leaving Cwm, cross Coast Path stile, not the private stile to Ty Canol Farm. Pause to admire the panoramic views behind you, from Carningli, through Newport to the estuary of the Nevern and northwards to Morfa Head. At Cat Rock marvellous views of Dinas Island and Cwm-yr-Eglwys appear. **In the days of the sea-quarries along the coast, the "cat-man" or tally-man used to sit on the peninsula counting the slate-carrying vessels as they moved in towards Parrog.**

Curlew.

11. Follow Coast Path to first cove at Aberrhigian. Perhaps pause awhile at this delightful unspoilt place. At the sign-post before the bridge follow the track straight on beside the stream. In case of difficulty cross and recross the river using the bridges.

12. The path proceeds through Cwm Rhigian woods, carpeted with bluebells, wild garlic and campion in the spring. This is a special place to walk all the year round, but can be very muddy!

13. Beyond the stile near Rhigian House, turn left up drive. At the junction of two tracks and a footpath, turn right up to the A487 trunk road.

14. Turn left at the trunk road. (Take care – there is fast moving traffic along this road and a blind corner to make matters worse.) Walk 200 m and then cross the road to enter farm track leading to Hendre. (Continue along trunk road for a shorter return route to Newport).

15. At the farm proceed straight ahead through two metal gates. After 100 m cross a stream and muddy path and turn sharp left into field. Follow the left hand hedge to a stile.

16. Cross stile and follow track straight ahead to another stile and thence to a third stile. This section of the walk is always wet underfoot; use banks if necessary.

17. Cross stile and strike straight up the slope to the corner of the wall about 20m ahead and follow path upwards to track between two walls and thence to Ffordd Bedd Morris. (The excellently preserved old Newport Cattle Pound can be visited with a minor deviation of about 100 m to the left just past the stile.) **This is where stray animals were impounded and released to their owners on payment of a fee. It has recently been rescued from the jungle and tidied up by a group of enthusiastic volunteers.**

18. Cross Ffordd Bedd Morris and take track between two houses, eventually joining a well marked track onto the open moorland.

19. Proceed straight ahead and follow this track for 1.5 km. The crags of Carn Ffoi are on your right as you enter the open moorland. **The summit was an important Iron Age fortified site, with powerful defensive ramparts enclosing a settlement platform. Also notice the derelict stone cottages which once made the mountainside a patchwork of small-holdings.** To the left is a marvellously unfolding panorama over the river, estuary, town, Pen Morfa and the sea.

20. Near Penwern you come to a junction at the metalled minor road. Proceed downhill over the cattle grid. **Note the old mill stream on the right and the Baptistry which is still in use. Just before Pont Henrietta Mair you can see the derelict Castle Mill, with the Castle itself being glimpsed through the trees. The mill was a corn-mill owned by the Lord Marcher of Cemais, and it was driven by water stored in the castle moat.**

THE ANCIENT GAME OF CNAPAN

One of Newport's strangest traditions is the Ancient Game of Cnapan, which was played on Traeth Mawr and on some of the large open fields of the Barony of Cemaes in the Sixteenth Century. The game is considered locally to be the real forerunner of rugby football, for it was a passing game in which the skills of evasive running, ball handling, and tackling were greatly admired. There were even episodes in the game which were similar to scrummages and lineouts.

Some of the great games attracted upwards of 2,000 players, and the "goals" were sometimes the porches of parish churches several miles apart. The games would last from dawn to dusk. The cnapan ball was made of solid wood, boiled in tallow to make it slippery. The gentry played in some of the games, mounted on horseback and armed with staves and cudgels. Not surprisingly, injuries were common, and the game was eventually banned. But it has been resurrected in Newport (in a more genteel form, strictly supervised by a referee!), and the Annual Cnapan Contest between Newport and Nevern parishes is now played during Spring Festival Week.

Newport Castle

41

Walking on the mountain.

21. At the bridge, proceed straight ahead, observing the twin cottages of Delfryn and Aelbryn on the left which were once a woollen mill, using water from the mill stream to drive the looms.

22. At the next junction you reach Bethlehem Chapel. Proceed across the road and take a short cut between the chapel and a cottage down to the A487 trunk road (Beware of traffic). Turn left along the main road for 50 m then right into Parrog Road. Pass Newport Pottery, one of two excellent craft establishments in Newport (the other is Acres Beach Gallery on the main road near Richards Bros Bus Depot). After 600 m you return to Parrog car-park.

A

LINKING ROUTES

1. Newport – Nevern – Bedd Morris – Newport. Follow Route Five instructions 1-10 and Route Three instructions 1-3, arriving at point (H). Then follow Route Five instructions 11-16. On reaching ruined Carningli Lodge turn right and follow track uphill, walking on common land. Turn left at corner and follow path all the way to Bedd Morris. Then follow Ffordd Bedd Morris seawards downhill to point (N), where you rejoin Route Six at point 18. Return to Newport as described.

2. Parrog – Bedd Morris – Parrog. Follow above route instructions 8-11, but then keep along Coast Path to Aberfforest. Now follow Route Seven instructions 10-16 to Bedd Morris. Follow Route Seven instructions 1-3. arriving at point (N). Turn right and follow above instructions 18-22 for return to the Parrog starting-point.

THE SEA QUARRIES
Many of the cliffs between Parrog and Cwm-yr-Eglwys have been affected by slate quarrying activities, and in the early 1800s the sea quarries were a hive of activity. Many of the quarries were owned by the Bowens of Llwyngwair. If you look carefully at the cliffs you can see the ledges, cuttings and spoil heaps left by the quarrymen. Some of the slate slabs were hauled up to the top of the cliffs, but most of them were taken down to sea-level and loaded into barges and small sailing vessels. Small "docks" were even cut into the rock face and used by vessels particularly at low tide. Many of the buildings of Newport were built with slabs of slate from these quarries, as were the sea walls and quays of the Parrog. The Parrog walls have recently been sensitively repaired by the local authorities.

BEDD MORRIS · ABERFFOREST · BEDD MORRIS

Starting from Bedd Morris car park (K), this is a fascinating circular route. It takes in a variety of landscapes, from windswept moorland to wooded valleys, and includes a short section along cliff tops. Parts of the route are wet and muddy, so please wear appropriate footwear. This is the most strenuous of all the routes in the booklet, involving a climb from sea-level to an altitude of 291 m, and it should only be attempted by those who are reasonably fit! There are two short cuts; the first can be used to create a short circular walk within a kilometre or so of Bedd Morris, and the second allows you to exclude the "coast and valley" section. Bus transport is available on the main road intersections. The route can be linked to Routes Four and Six and can be extended even further east beyond Newport.

DIRECTIONS

K 1. Start at Bedd Morris car park on the Newport-Pontfaen road. Follow road downhill for 1 km towards Newport, and then turn left at signpost above first small coniferous plantation. *This is classic "smallholding country" with little stone-walled fields, sheep enclosures, and ruined cottages in abundance. The colours and textures of the landscape in this area make it a paradise for painters and photographers.*

2. Follow track down over moorland then between walls and fields. Keep left at first track junction, and continue down walled track to veer right to farm access road near seat. (Here if you want to complete a short circular walk, you can turn left instead. Follow track past farms, and on reaching signpost at cross-tracks, turn left and return to Bedd Morris.) Turn right to follow road down past houses (and converted chapel) for about 1 km to road T-junction.

N 3. Turn left at junction, and proceed down road for a short distance. Immediately after small coniferous plantation on left, turn left at

ROUTE SEVEN

DISTANCE
CIRCULAR WALK OF 11 KM (C 7 MILES).

TIME
4 HRS WITHOUT STOPS.

DIFFICULTY
STRENUOUS.

PLACES OF INTEREST
BEDD MORRIS, OLD CATTLE POUND, ABERRHIGIAN, ABERFFOREST, OLD GREEN WAY.

PARKING
CAR PARKS AT BEDD MORRIS, NEAR PONT NEWYDD (LAY-BY). ROADSIDE PARKING AT FFORDD BEDD MORRIS.

TRANSPORT
BUS STOPPING PLACES ON A487 AT PONT NEWYDD AND PONT FELIN WERN-DEW.

MAPS
OS 1:50,000 LANDRANGER SERIES SHEET 145; OS 1:25,000 PATHFINDER SERIES 1033.

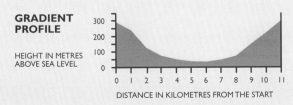

GRADIENT PROFILE

HEIGHT IN METRES ABOVE SEA LEVEL

DISTANCE IN KILOMETRES FROM THE START

signpost to follow muddy walled track down into field. Keep along the path parallel to wall. (Ignore path to right unless you wish to visit the Old Cattle Pound).

4. At corner of wall, veer right to stile over wall at bottom of field. Cross stile and keep straight ahead on track. (This section can be very wet – keep to banks at side of track if necessary). Follow track down to next stile, and cross into field. Follow green lane (wet and muddy) to gate and second stile, and cross into next field. Please keep to field edge on right.

5. At bottom of field, turn right through opening and ford stream. Again this is very wet and muddy; keep to left side to cross. Proceed along farm track to gate. Continue past farm house (Hendre), and along concrete drive to main road.

6. Cross main road, and then turn left to follow grass verge along to farm access road on right. (For a shorter circular walk, avoiding cliff path, proceed along main road to west. Then follow instructions 12 – 16 to return to Bedd Morris). *(About 200m to the west, along the main road, just past Pont Newydd bridge and the house on the right, there is a field gate. In the field you can see a Neolithic burial chamber (Cerrig y Gof) which is unique in the British Isles. It has no less than five connected chambers in which burial remains were found).* Otherwise continue down Aberrhigian access road towards house (Rhigian).

7. Immediately before house, turn right onto path to cross stile. Follow path down lane into woods, to cross muddy section before reaching path junction before waterfall.

8. Turn right at path junction, and follow path down through woods and alongside stream. Sections of this path can be very muddy. Continue down to sea at Aberrhigian Bay, and cross old bridge to pebble beach.*This is one of the most interesting pebble beaches in Pembrokeshire, with colourful pebbles from many parts of the western seaboard of Britain dumped here by a melting glacier during the last glacial episode about 15,000 years ago. Some of the "erratic" pebbles have even come from Scotland.*

M 9. Turn left to cross beach, then ascend steps to follow coast path towards next bay (Aberfforest). This path follows the cliff tops – please take care, and keep young children and dogs under strict control.

L 10. After stile descend steps to Aberfforest Bay. *Note the horsetail plants adjacent to the path; these plants thrive in sticky calcareous clay soils, and they are among the most primitive plants in the world. They are closely related to the gigantic "tree horsetails" which thrived in the Coal Measures forests over 300 million years ago.* At bottom stile, turn left to follow access road uphill towards buildings. In a short distance, turn left to follow waymarked path up field alongside fence, and proceed up to access road at top. Turn left at access road, and proceed past farm up to main road.

Buzzard.

THE MOORLANDS
The bleak but colourful moorlands of Carningli and Mynydd Dinas are very important both ecologically and economically. Because of high rainfall, exposure and acid soils, tree growth is inhibited, and the typical vegetation is open grassland interspersed with patches of heather moor. On the wetter areas cotton grass and rushes predominate, and on the mountain flanks there is much gorse, hawthorn, rowan and bracken. Buzzards, kestrels and ravens can be seen wheeling or hanging in the high winds. One of the reasons for the lack of trees on the common is the ancient practice of animal grazing; both sheep and ponies help to maintain the characteristic vegetation. Commoners grazing rights are under the jurisdiction of the Court Leet. Patches of the moorland are burnt by local farmers every year, keeping heather under control and encouraging new grass growth. In the old days peat was also cut from parts of the moorland.

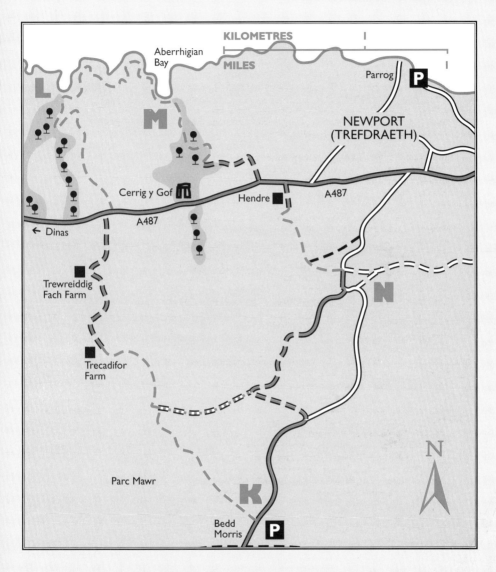

11. At main road, cross then turn right for short way to access road on left.

12. At entrance to farm access road, turn left and follow road to Trewreiddig Fach farm. At farm, turn left to continue on farm lane uphill towards second farm.

13. At second farm (Trecadifor), keep left at entrance to follow grassy and muddy track up to gate. Continue on track uphill, veering left at first track junction. Continue uphill, bearing left at

Wild garlic in bloom.

second track junction towards wooden gate into walled track. *This is a classic local example of a "green way", used as a route for domesticated animals ever since the Iron Age.*

14. Continue along sunken walled track uphill, passing through gate before reaching cross-tracks. Keep straight ahead and uphill, to gate at edge of moorland.

15. Follow track across moorland, passing rock outcrop to left. *These are the Parc Mawr tors, typical of the outcrops of dolerite and other volcanic rocks that give the upland landscape much of its character. The moorland is littered with frost-shattered rocky crags and glacial erratics (boulders left behind about 14,000 years ago at the end of the last glacial episode).*

16. Continue along moorland track to road, then turn right to return to Bedd Morris car park.

LINKING ROUTES

1. Bedd Morris – Newport. If you wish to complete a one-way walk from Bedd Morris to Newport, follow instructions 1-2 as far as (N) and then turn right. Follow instructions 18-22 on Route Six, finishing the walk at the Parrog car park.

2. Bedd Morris – Newport via Coast Path. This is a longer walk which takes in a beautiful stretch of the Coast Path. Follow instructions 1-8 to Aberrhigian, turn right at (M) and follow Coast Path to Parrog.

ABERFFOREST
This little creek has been used by local farmers and fishermen for many centuries, since it has a sandy bottom and is well sheltered from the westerly winds. Small sailing vessels could enter with care, carrying general cargoes but more especially anthracite and limestone for the lime kiln at the head of the bay. Fishermen kept their small sailing boats here until quite recent times, but now the most hectic nautical activity is associated with pleasure craft. Like many of the small ports and harbours strung along the Pembrokeshire coast, Aberfforest has been given a new lease of life by the holiday industry, and on a fine summers day pleasure craft of all sorts can be seen here and at Parrog and Cwm-yr-Eglwys.

OTHER WALKS

The Carningli Walks area is now well served by walks published in a variety of different formats. The pioneering local walks booklet was *Looking Around Newport,* edited by D. Islwyn Jenkins and published in 1970. It contained ten walks which are still well worth following (if you can find a copy of the booklet, which is long since out of print). In 1989 David Vaughan published a series of six *Newport Walks* designed for families. These walks included a number of the routes described in the present booklet. In the same year the NPA published *Six Circular Walks Around Newport* by Brian John; these were produced as a series of laminated cards in a plastic folder. The NPA booklet *Walking in the Presely Hills* (again by Brian John) includes descriptions for three routes which impinge on the Carningli – Cwm Gwaun area. The same author's *Pembrokeshire Coast Path National Trail Guide* (Aurum Press) describes the Coast Path between Cemaes Head and Dinas Island, and there are a number of other publications by Tony Roberts and other authors which cover the same coastal territory. The most detailed description of the coastal route is in Christopher John Wright's *Guide to the Pembrokeshire Coast Path.* A new addition to the inland literature is Brian John's *Five Circular Walks: Gwaun Valley East,* published in 1995 by the NPA. The routes described are relatively short, but they give a fine impression of the countryside to the south of the hill mass of Carningli.

BLUESTONE COUNTRY

The Carningli Walks area is part of the upland spine of north Pembrokeshire, closely related to the main hill mass of the Preseli Hills but distinct in that it brings upland scenery to within a couple of kilometres of the sea. The Preseli Tourist Association, in conjunction with Preseli Pembrokeshire District Council and the Wales Tourist Board, has designated this upland area "Bluestone Country" since the most important rock type to be found here is a blue-grey dolerite. Most of the crags and carns are made of bluestone, often weather-beaten and encrusted with brightly-coloured lichens. Even away from the rock outcrops, boulders of dolerite project through the moorland blanket of heather and grassland. The stone is also the most valuable and durable building stone throughout north Pembrokeshire; and it is used over hundreds of square kilometres for the building of stone walls, for gateposts and lintels, steps and sills.

Another link makes the term "Bluestone Country" particularly evocative: namely the link with the Bluestone Circle at Stonehenge. Most of the remaining bluestones arranged inside the massive trilithons at Stonehenge come from the Preseli Hills area; some of them are made of a peculiar "spotted dolerite" which is most characteristic of the Carn Meini area at the eastern end of the upland ridge. Whether these stones were taken to Stonehenge by glacier ice or by Neolithic men is immaterial; the most important point is that some sort of link between Preseli and Stonehenge is now accepted by geologists and archaeologists alike.

ACKNOWLEDGEMENTS

The Carningli Walks series was devised by the Footpaths Committee of the Carningli Rural Initiative (CRI) with the intention of encouraging both local residents and visitors to make use of the area's superb network of footpaths and bridleways. The identification, clearing and marking of these routes has occupied many local people and organizations over a period of 15 years or more, and there are many who deserve our thanks. We thank the Newport and Nevern Community Councils for instigating much of the route identification work; in particular we are grateful for the long and continuing interest of Miss Vida Davies and Mr Jimmy Williams. We thank the Board of CRI under the chairmanship of Maureen Bennett for constant encouragement and for its fund-raising efforts. We thank the many local landowners who have cooperated over the installation of stiles and waymarks and on route clearance. The first phase of the Carningli Walks project was opened with due ceremony by the TV chef Keith Floyd in 1992. With funding from the WDA Rural Prosperity Programme and with the close support and involvement of the NPA and Preseli Pembrokeshire District Council, a walks leaflet was produced and promoted nationally through the media. The leaflet was printed by Preseli Pembrokeshire DC with the kind support of Tourism Officer Richard Howells. It received a very favourable response from the public, but because of budgetary constraints it suffered from a lack of detailed maps and route descriptions. However, the exercise served to open up a number of new routes and to introduce them to a new generation of countryside walkers.

The present booklet is the culmination of work on Phase Two of the Project. In particular, we are happy to acknowledge that this is a joint enterprise which would not have been possible without the generous involvement of the Pembrokeshire Coast National Park Department and the Welsh Development Agency. On the NPA side, particular thanks are due to Peter Hordley, local ranger Geraint Harries, and Tom Goodall and his staff who have been responsible for so much of the waymarking, stile building and footpath maintenance work. We thank Brian Jones and Helen Evans for their invaluable support in the CRI office. The other members of the CRI Footpaths Committee (Vicky Rodden, Stanley Morrow, and Tim Muntz) have given many hours of their time. We also thank Leon Olin for his illustrations, John Havard for his photography, Jack Jackson of Brace-Harvatt Associates for his design expertise, and Haven Colourprint for printing work. We also thank Gordon Reed of the WDA for his continuing personal support for the project.

Peter Harwood, Robin Evans,
Brian John and David Vaughan.   February 1995.